# Guide to Finding a Loyalist Ancestor in Upper Canada (Ontario)

## by
## Lorine McGinnis Schulze

Publisher Olive Tree Genealogy
ISBN 978-1-987938-26-5

# What is a Loyalist?

A Loyalist is any person who is loyal to their allegiance (especially in times of revolt). During the American Revolution (Revolutionary War) in what was to become the United States of America, a Loyalist (also called UEL which stands for United Empire Loyalist) was anyone who remained loyal to the King of England.

When the American Revolution began in 1775, individuals living in the 13 British colonies had to decide whether to remain loyal to the British King or to fight for independence. *Loyalist* is the term used to describe those who supported the King and who later fled to Canada with their families. You may sometimes see Loyalists referred to as *Tories* but this is not the commonly accepted term. Most Loyalists fled to Canada and helped settle that country, particularly in what is now Ontario and Nova Scotia.

## Lands Confiscated

Loyalists were harassed socially and politically. Many were expelled from their land and their property was seized. Many were arrested. One Loyalist ancestor living near North River, New York was arrested and in 1779 his home was burned to the ground forcing his family to flee to Montreal Canada. My Loyalist ancestor from New Jersey did not take up arms but remained sympathetic to the British forces and according to official documents

*"[he] suffered greatly both in his person and property in the Late War between Great Britain and America"*

## Fleeing to Canada

The first trickle of Loyalists into Canada was in March 1776 when 1000 people fled Boston and accompanied the British Army as it retreated before the American forces. In 1782 when the Revolution ended, Canada consisted of two colonies: Quebec and Nova Scotia. Approximately 10,000 Loyalists went to Quebec, the rest to Nova Scotia.

## Quebec Settlements

Those who settled in Quebec ran into problems with the French feudal system of land ownership and agitated for the creation of an English-speaking province. As a result, the Quebec colony was divided into Upper and Lower Canada in 1791. Loyalists came overland to the Niagara Peninsula in the new area of Upper Canada.

## Ontario Settlements

Although there were exceptions, Loyalist settlement in 1784 in what is now the Province of  Ontario  was mostly by discharged servicemen from Ranger Units who settled in roughly the following pattern, going from east to west along the St. Lawrence River and Lake Ontario:

* Lancaster Township: Royal Yorkers settled there in 1785
* Charlottenburgh Township: Roman Catholic Highlanders in the Royal Yorkers
* Cornwall Township: Scottish Presbyterians in the Royal Yorkers
* Osnabruck Township: German Calvinists in the Royal Yorkers
* Williamsburgh Township: German Lutherans in the Royal Yorkers
* Matilda Township: Anglicans in the Royal Yorkers
* Edwardsburgh, Augusta and Elizabethtown Townships: Major Jessup's Loyal Rangers
* Kingston Township: Captain Michael Grass and his New York

Loyalists
* Ernestown Township: Jessup's Rangers
* Fredericksburgh Township: Major James Rogers' Co. of the **King's Rangers** and the 2nd Battalion of the Royal Yorkers
* Adolphustown Township: DeLancey's Corps
* Marysburgh Township: German mercenaries and disbanded English and Irish troops
* Sophiasburgh Township: Americans who arrived after the Revolution
* Ameliasburgh Township: no specific Loyalist units
* Sidney Township: no specific Loyalist units
* Niagara Region: **Butler's Rangers**

# Land Grants

By 1784, Loyalists could return to America without fear of persecution or physical assault, and some did. Those who stayed in Canada were granted land under the following conditions:

* 100 acres for head of family plus 50 acres per family member
* 50 acres for single men
* 300 to 1000 acres for army officers
* 200 acres for a Non-commissioned officer plus 200 for wives, if they applied
* 100 acres for a private soldier plus 50 acres for each family member

In order to obtain their grant of land, an individual had to meet certain requirements (which changed slightly depending on the year of application):

- had to live in the American colonies before the start of the American Revolution
- joined the  British forces before 1783
- suffered property losses

In 1798 a fourth requirement was added, that an individual had to be living in Upper Canada before 1798

Lots were drawn for locations and when the land had been occupied for a year, the Loyalist received a permanent deed. In 1789, it was decided that sons would receive 200 acres when they became 21 and daughters the same, except they would receive the grant upon marriage if not yet 21. This was known as an Order in Council which you may see referred to as OIC.

For instance here is a one-line entry for one of my Loyalist Ancestors, found in Reid's book *The Loyalists in Ontario: The Sons and Daughters of the American Loyalists of Upper Canada.* The entry reads:

*Cornelius Vollick OIC 25 May 1793*

This brief entry tells us that Cornelis received his land grant on 25 May 1793. Since I know his father was a Loyalist I also know that Cornelis was at least 21 years old in 1793. Therefore I know he was born 1772 or earlier. This also tells me that he submitted a petition to receive his Loyalist Land Grant, and so I need to look for that petition. I may get a surprise as it is possible he was applying for land in right of being a confirmed Loyalist himself and not just a son of a confirmed Loyalist. The Petition, if found, will have the information as to under what conditions he was applying.

# Land Boards of Upper Canada, 1765-1804

The Land Boards were established in 1789 to oversee land matters, settle the four districts (Hesse, Nassau, Lunenburg and Mecklenburg, all of which later became Upper Canada) and to grant land to the settlers. Settlers were given free land, rations, farm stock and farm implements. Lands were also granted to the sons and daughters of Loyalists. In 1794 the Land Boards were abolished.

However you will find some earlier land records dating back to 1765 and a few later ones as late as 1804.

There is a searchable index for the Land Board records online at Library and Archives Canada website. After finding a name of interest you can consult the filmed documents

The Land Board records include:

- minutes
- reports
- correspondence
- instructions or regulations for the operation of the Land Boards
- schedules of locations and of lands granted
- oaths of allegiance

# Upper Canada Land Petitions (UCLP) 1763-1865

Every individual who believed they were entitled to a grant of land under Loyalist Regulations, had to file a petition with the Executive Council. In their petition the individual presented their case for receiving a grant. These Land Petitions often contain a wealth of genealogical information.

The petition of Storm Folluck (above) is a typical petition. Petitions could consist of many pages submitted by one individual. This petition states (in formal language)

*The Petition of Storm Folluck Humbly Sheweth That your petitioner served as a Private in Col. Butler's Corps, that as yet your Petitioner has only drawn from His Majesty's 200 acres, most of which your Petitioner has improved, therefore prays your Honour will be pleased to grant him an additional 100 acres to put him on a footing with other soldiers of that corps.*

There is the formal typical ending of *"... as in Duty bound your Petitioner will ever pray"* and dated Niagara January 1797

☐Some petitions are as little as one page outlining military service. Some are many pages long and often include affidavits from commanding officers testifying to military service. Sometimes affidavits or letters are included which outline personal hardships and suffering in the American Colonies - arrests, property seized, homes burned, and so on. If an individual applied for a land grant as the son or daughter of an approved Loyalist, reference is made to the Loyalist parent. You never know what you will find in a petition until you read it.

**Where to Find a Land Petition**

Library & Archives Canada has indexed the UCLP (Upper Canada Land Petitions), and genealogists can now search the index on the LAC website. If you find a name of interest in the index, be sure you copy the details exactly as you will need the Microfilm Number, Volume Number, Bundle Letter and Number, and the Petition Number.

The Volume, Bundle and Petition numbers and letters allow you to find the Petition(s) you want on the microfilm reel. You can view the digitized microfilms online on Library and Archives Canada. Remember that Upper Canada is now present day Ontario. Also it is important to note that the UCLP (Upper Canada Land Petitions) include petitions from individuals other than Loyalists.

Once a petition was submitted, it was read in Council and a decision was made. Whether the individual's petition was recommended (approved) or denied is marked on the outside "envelope" of the petition.

This is the dated Order in Council (OIC) and it will have a brief reference to how much land was granted and under what regulations, or the fact that the petition was denied.

# An Example of a Land Petition from a Loyalist

The affidavit above is part of a large bundle of letters, affidavits, and petitions from my Loyalist ancestor Isaac Vollick which he submitted in 1797. Each bundle is given a number, in this case "27". Then each page in that specific bundle is assigned a letter. The affidavit is 27K indicating that A, B, C, D, E, F, G, H, I and J preceeded it. You can see that this set of papers for Isaac probably contains a great deal of interesting information.

This specific piece of his petition in 1797 states

*I do hereby certify that Isaac Volek [sic] served in Butler's Rangers from the year 1778 to the end of the War. That his wife and family suffered much during his absence [xxx] were sent prisoners a considerable distance from home.*

*Newark March 30th 1797 [signed] J. Ball, JP*

*Isaac Volck's [sic] wife came to Niagara in the year 1782.*

*J. Ball*

I have learned a great deal from this one piece of paper among many - that Isaac was in Butler's Rangers from 1778 on. That his family were imprisoned and then exiled. That his wife (and probably children) arrived in Niagara in 1782.

# Understanding Notations on the Envelope of an Upper Canada Land Petition

It is important to read and save the "envelope" for any petitions you find, as the envelopes tell us what the final outcome was to the petitioner's request.

Above you see the envelope for the petition of Abraham DeForest. Abraham's petition was a fairly simple one page request. He asked for extra lands as a Loyalist, above and beyond the lands he had previously received.

The envelope provides his abbreviated name (Ab. Deforest) followed by this note:

*"Recommended for 100 acres in addition to the lot he has received as family lands if it is apparent from the Surveyor General Books he is entitled to them*

*Read in Council*
*August 12, 1795"*

Then follows a darker notation *"V Ent. P 299"* This refers to the Land Book where the entry for Abraham's lands can be found. Sometimes there is more detail in these Land Books but often it is simply a summary notation of the petitioner's name and land.

An envelope for Abraham's wife Elizabeth Bowman is a bit more complex and has several notations in different handwriting. First, the numbers at the top of an envelope refer to the Volume, Bundle and Petition number which we talked about in my first post on finding the petitions.

Next the words *"Petition of Elizabeth Deforest for land as D.U.E."* D.U.E. stands for *"Daughter of United Empire Loyalist"* which tells us that Elizabeth's father was a recognized Loyalist. As such Elizabeth was entitled to a free grant of land. If she were a male, it would read *"S.U.E."* or *"Son of a United Empire Loyalist"*

The next notation reads

*"Received 28th January 1817 from Abraham Bowman"* and is signed by the Clerk John B-----

In lighter handwriting is the notation *"DUE"* and the signature of an official. It appears the Council recognized that Elizabeth was a DUE.

A sideways notation reads *"Entered in Land Book J, page 110"* and the final legible notation in dark ink reads

*"Referred to the Council by His Excellency this day and Recommended 8th March. Read and granted 26th march 1817"*

This tells us that Elizabeth received the lands she requested. Elizabeth's petition consisted of several pages. On one page she filled out a pre-written form stating she was the daughter of Jacob Bowman, a Loyalist, that she was married to Abraham Deforest and had never received the land grant she was entitled to as the daughter of a Loyalist. Also included was an affidavit from the Justice of the Peace stating that Elizabeth had appeared before the Magistrates and was accepted as the daughter of Jacob Bowman, Loyalist

# Upper Canada Land Books

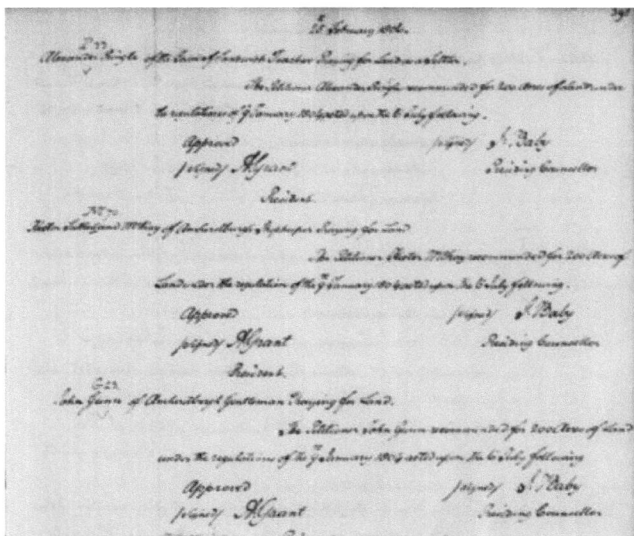

The Upper Canada Land Books do not, for the most part, contain much more information than the names of petitioners for land. Above is a typical page from those books.

If you cannot find your ancestor in a Land Petition, you may find his or her name in the Land Books. Sometimes more detail is found in the comments section of the Land Book reference, but not often. Library & Archives Canada provides a list of microfilm reel numbers for both Upper and Lower Canada Land Books.

There are four Land Books for Upper Canada (A, B, C & D) which are in chronological order from 17 February 1787 to 13 July 1798.

The Upper Canada Land Book C covering 11 April to 20 December 1797 has been indexed and abstracted and can be consulted online. There are also some out-of-order petition entries for June and July 1796 in this database.

There are also Upper Canada Land Books up to 1841 which have been name-indexed by the Ontario Genealogical Society (OGS), the entire list being available on a CD from OGS. Loyalists continued to petition the government (and thus Land Book entries) at least until the mid-nineteenth century.

An example of a Land Book entry is one for my ancestor Jacob Peer in July 1797. His one line entry in Land Book C states

*"Peer, Jacob - Praying for lands as a settler. Recommended for 200 acres."*

That is a typical entry. However some entries provide much more detail such as this one for Rebecca Seeley

*"Seeley, Rebecca - Praying for 3000 acres of lands in remuneration of her father's losses during the American war. The committee of Council are restricted from recommending lands as a compensation for losses, commissioners having been sent by His Majesty to this country for the especial purpose of remunerating the suffering loyalists. As the petitioner appears to have neglected this opportunity, the committee regret that they can only recommend her for 200 acres, if her father's name appears on the U.E. List."*

Remember - these are brief entries from the Land Books.

Petitions in the Upper Canada Land Petition files contain letters, affidavits, petitions, oaths of allegiance and more.

# Land Petitions of Lower Canada, 1764-1841

Lower Canada before 1791 included what is now Ontario as well as what is now Quebec. It is therefore worth searching these records to see if your ancestor's petition for land is there.

These records are also online at Library and Archives Canada website.

# CLRI (Computerized Land Records Index)

CLRI (Computerized Land Records Index) (aka Ontario Land Record Index) summarizes land grants from sales of Crown Land, from Canada Company sales or leases and from Peter Robinson settlers' grants. If your ancestor settled anywhere in Ontario and he was the first time buyer of Crown Land, he will be on these lists. Loyalists were the first time owners of Crown Lands and thus are almost always found in the CLRI.

The information from the CLRI one-line entry includes date of purchase, type of purchase, residence of purchaser, land location (lot, concession, township), type of purchase (very important to knowing whether or not there are more records available!), archival reference (where full record can be found) and often more info such as date of land ticket, or date of petition for land, etc.

The CLRI can be accessed in many Ontario Libraries. You can also request a lookup in this database at
http://www.olivetreegenealogy.com/can/ont/clri.shtml

# Loyalist Lists

There is no one list of Loyalists, and it is a misconception to think that there is. There are lists of approved Loyalists, but there was more than one created by different agencies. They are all different in varying ways, and there is no list that is considered the final word.

For example the Crown Lands Department created lists of Loyalists based on a variety of sources. This is the Crown Lands List (aka Old UEL List). It contains approximately 6,000 names but only about half are qualified UEL.

The Executive Council devised a different list from various district rolls. This list is called the Executive Council UE List. This list, considered more accurate than the Old UEL List, contains about 3,000 names but is not complete.

Both these lists, which were first drawn up in the 1790s, have been altered since they were written. The important thing to remember is that if you consult these lists, a negative result (your ancestor's name does not appear) does not necessarily mean he is not a qualified Loyalist!

The United Empire Loyalist Lists [NA RG 1, L7 vol 52a] is available in book form; and as microfilm -- United Empire Loyalist Lists [NA RG 1, L7 Vol 52a] on C-2222 from the Ontario Archives

There are also the Inspector General's Loyalist registers. There are three registers (or lists) with names of Loyalist claimants in Upper Canada. The lists were created to provide a comprehensive listing of United Empire Loyalists, their sons and daughters, who were entitled to free grants of land. Two of the lists were compiled from the rolls drawn up by the District Land Boards on the order of Lieutenant-Governor Simcoe beginning in 1796. From 1798 to 1839, additions and exclusions were made to the lists. The third list was compiled from muster rolls.

Some original muster rolls of Loyalist corps and provision lists are found in the Haldimand Papers and British Headquarters Papers, formerly the Carleton Papers.

It is important to note that there is overlap in these lists. Researchers will want to consult all of them in order to be certain nothing was overlooked in the search for a Loyalist ancestor.

There is also William D. Reid's book *The Loyalists in Ontario: The Sons and Daughters of the American Loyalists of Upper Canada*

While Reid's book is an excellent starting point in your Loyalist research you must use it with caution. There are errors and omissions. Reid did not always group families together correctly. There are many family members who have been left out. He did not find every single Loyalist and list them in the book.

So if you do not find an ancestor in the book, it doesn't prove he was not a Loyalist. Don't accept family groups without verification. However if you find an ancestor with an OIC date, that means Reid saw that there was a petition on file for that person and you should consult the Upper Canada Land Petitions which we talked about in Chapter 3.

The first place you should look for a possible Loyalist ancestor is in the land records, because Loyalists and their families were granted land in accordance with their military rank and dependents.

# Inspector General's Loyalist Registers

The Ontario Archives holds the Inspector General's Loyalist Registers. The Office of the Inspector General was responsible for determining if applicants for land grants were privileged. These records consist of three registers listing the names of Loyalist claimants in Upper Canada. The lists were created to provide a comprehensive listing of United Empire Loyalists, and their sons and daughters, who were entitled to free grants of land.

The three registers are:
* Volume RG 1-515-0-0-1 compiled from the rolls drawn up by the District Land Boards on the order of Lieutenant-Governor Simcoe beginning in 1796
* Volume RG 1-515-0-0-2 compiled from the rolls drawn up by the District Land Boards on the order of Lieutenant-Governor Simcoe beginning in 1796
* Volume RG 1-515-0-0-3 compiled from muster rolls.

# Crown Lands List (aka Old UEL List)

## APPENDIX B.

Copy of the " Old U. E. List," preserved in the Crown Lands Department at Toronto.

### KEY TO ABBREVIATIONS.

S.B.R.—Soldier in Butler's Rangers
K.R.R. or R.R.—Is Royl. Regt. N. York.
p. P.—Is p. their Petition.
l .R.—Is Loyal Rangers.
Q. R.—Queen's Rangers.
L. Bd. L.—The Land Board of Lunenburg.
R.L.B.S.—Return Land Board Stormont.
L.B.M.—Land Board Mecklenburg.

L.B.A.—Land Board Adolphustown.
L.B.K.—Land Board of Kingston.
P.L.—Provision List Kingston.
P.L.N.J.—Provision List New Johnstowne.
P.L 2d.—Provision List Eastern District.
P.L.N.—Provision List Niagara.
B.M.A.—Capt. Barnes' Muster Absentees.

| NAMES. | RESIDENCE. | DESCENDANTS. |
|---|---|---|
| Abbott, Joseph ...... | W. District............ | Sergeant, disched. from the 26th Regmt., his own Petition in C.O. |
| Abney, Jonas ........ | Ernest Town.......... | No person of this name on the roll. |
| Abraham, Christian .. | Do.  ............ | Soldier R.R.N.Y. Called Loyalist P. L. 1786. |

You will find a published list of Loyalists on pages 129-280 of Appendix B in the online book *The centennial of the settlement of Upper Canada by the United Empire Loyalists, 1784-1884; the celebrations at Adolphustown, Toronto and Niagara, with an appendix, containing a copy of the U.E. List, preserved in the Crown Lands Department at Toronto"* on Archives.org

There is a second list in this same online book on page 281 called "Names Inserted on the U.E. List by order of the Honourable the Executive Council" From page 282 to page 332 is a third list titled "Supplementary List". The Supplementary List is not in alphabetical order.

# Petition of 547 Loyalists From New York City 1776

This is a miscellaneous list of Loyalists in a petition they filed on November 28, 1776. The list can be viewed as online images at the New York Historical Archives website. The images are found under New York Heritage Digital Collections.

According to the website: "Also known as the 'Loyalist declaration of dependence', this was the second petition addressed to the Royal Commissioners Richard and William Howe from loyalists seeking special protection under British occupation. Their first petition, for the suspension of martial law, went unanswered; in this second, insisting that they had risked their lives and fortunes opposing 'the most unnatural, unprovoked rebellion, that ever disgraced the annals of time', the loyalists sought only 'some level of distinction' from the 'inhabitants in general'. Little improved for the loyalists, however, and they suffered additionally from the demoralizing effects of inflation, wartime profiteering, street violence, and general dirt and stench."

# The Haldimand Papers

These important papers were kept by Sir Frederick Haldimand, 1718-1791. The papers document events in North America beginning with the Seven Years War and ending with the settlement by Loyalists after the American Revolutionary War. The image above is a 1783 list of Loyalists who settled at Niagara, Upper Canada (present day Ontario) along with the number of household members (recorded by gender and age). It is an example of what you might find for an ancestor in the Haldimand Papers.

Finding an ancestor in the digitized records is a challenge but it can be done and the wealth of information is incredible. The first thing you need to know is that although the papers themselves have not been transcribed or indexed, there is an overlooked index to Loyalists found on Heritage Canada's digitized microfilm C-1475.

When you consult this typed index you will see the individual Loyalist's name followed by a set of numbers. Warning: the film is blurry!

Laraway, Jonas

105, p.72
167, p.111,314,314,319,379
168, p.40,72

This is the index showing one of my Loyalist ancestors, Jonas Larroway. Note the alternate spelling of his surname. The 3-digit number that you see first is the Volume number. That is where you will find the original record for the individual. Following the 3-digit volume number is the page (or pages) number. The image above shows that Jonas Larroway has documents in three different volumes. I want to find the 5 pages for Jonas Larroway in Volume 167.

Sounds easy, right? Wouldn't we just go to whatever film holds Volume 167 and then look for the pages? How I wish it were that easy but it's not. There are 43 digitized films for the Haldimand Papers on Heritage Canada website but there is no explanation of what is found in each film. So we do not know what film holds Volume 167.

Checking Library and Archives Canada to find out what film holds Volume 167 also comes up empty. There is nothing found that describes the films, or provides a description of them. To complicate things, there are different naming and numbering systems assigned to the films, depending on who labelled them, and when. Since the microfilm copies of the Additional Manuscripts in the Loyalist Collection and the Transcript volumes in Library and Archives Canada are not identical, you are going to need a conversion chart to understand what film you need. I'm going to explain where and how to get that chart but first I need to explain the various labelling systems you're going to find on the conversion chart.

The original Haldimand Papers are in the British Library and are labelled British Library Additional Manuscripts (Add MSS) 21,661 - 21,892 inclusive. Library and Archives Canada uses the Series B transcripts (H-followed by 4 digits), the Series B transcript volume numbers (B-followed by 3 digits). You will also see the World Microfilm Publishing (WMP) film number of the actual papers on the conversion chart.

The Volume number is equivalent to a B film number. So in the example above where we saw 5 pages for Jonas Larroway in Volume 167, we know we need to find B-167. But we still don't know what film it is on. It took me an entire day to figure out what films I needed. Once I figured it out, I found an impressive set of miscellaneous papers with my ancestors' names receiving rations from the British Government, on Loyalist Muster rolls and more.

Here are the steps you need to take to find your own ancestor!

## Step 1

First consult the index found on Haldimand Papers Microfilm C-1475 on Heritage Canada. Four bound volumes of transcripts (V 165, V 166, V 167, V 168) which relate primarily to Loyalists, together with a typed index have been microfilmed on this film. The index is near the start of the film and it is in alphabetical order by surname. Find your name of interest and copy the Volume Number (aka B number) and all pages listed.

You may find it easier to download a typed index which is identical to the rather blurry images of the index found on C-1475. This typed index is found on Collections Canada as a PDF file which you can save to your computer. This is the link for the index
http://data2.archives.ca/pdf/pdf001/p000002411.pdf

I should mention that you would be wise to avoid looking for any filmed records (other than the index) in C-1475. The C films are very bad quality and are difficult to read, having been filmed in the 1950s. The H films were filmed in the 1980s and are much better quality.

## Step 2

| H-1654 | | B-167 | 21827 to page 320 | 85 |
| | | | Nominal index LAC site or film C-1475 | |
| H-1655 | #35 | B-167 | 21827 from page 321 | 85 |
| | | | Nominal index LAC site or film C-1475 | |

Consult the PDF conversion chart found online which gives conversions from B numbers to the correct film. The author of the chart created the following columns: LAC (Library and Archives Canada) reel; Batch #s; B series; Add MSS; WMP reel # This conversion chart allows you to convert the Library and Archives films of the Series B transcripts (H-followed by 4 numbers), the Series B transcript volume numbers (B-followed by 3 numbers), the Add MSS 4-digit numbers from the British Library and the WMP (World Microfilm Publishing) film number of the actual papers.

You can download the chart by using this link:
http://freepages.genealogy.rootsweb.ancestry.com/%7Esay lormowbray/haldimandchart.pdf

So for example looking for B-167 on the Conversion Chart we see that B-167 is found on 2 films, H-1654 and H-1655. Ignore the 21827 as that is the Add MSS number. The important fact here is that B-167 pages 1 to 320 are found on H-1654. Caveat: Those pages will be found at the end of that film, not the beginning. There are other Volumes (B numbers) at the beginning of the film. Then pages 321 to the end were filmed on H-1655.

## Step 3

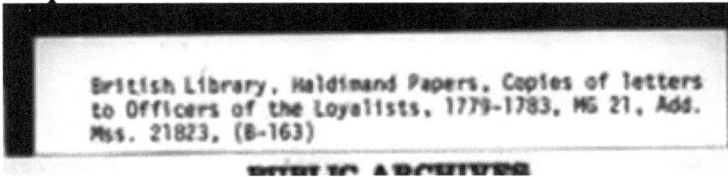

British Library, Haldimand Papers, Copies of letters to Officers of the Loyalists, 1779-1783, MG 21, Add. Mss. 21823, (B-163)

Go to the list of Haldimand Papers digitized films on Canadiana.org and scroll down to H-1654. Start the film and note what volume (B number) you are viewing. You can see the source details at the bottom or right hand side of each filmed page as illustrated in the above image.

Once you reach your volume (B number) of interest, simply look for the page numbers you want. You will then find information on your Loyalist ancestor.

# Calendar

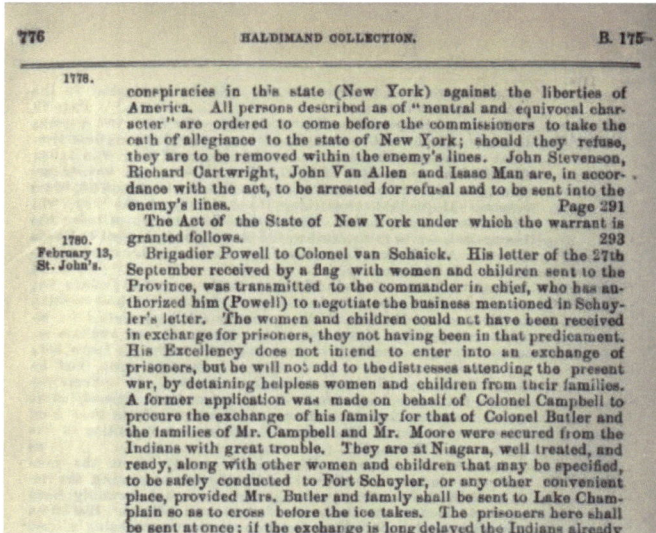

There is also a Calendar for the Haldimand Papers which was published in *Report on Public Archives of Canada*, editions 1884 to 1889. Every document found in the Haldimand Papers is listed, along with a brief description. While you will not find lists of Loyalists you will find reference to various men and women, as well as wonderful descriptions of events.

For example, a search for "Niagara" brought up dozens of results. One was the reference in the image above, which mentions the families of Mr. Moore and Mr. Campbell being released from the Indians and now safe at Niagara. At the top of the page is the Volume number where more details may be found (B-175) Another search for the term "Loyalists" indicates that on B-168, p. 752 there is a "Return of Loyalists desiring to settle in Canada, 1784" All I have to do is find the film for B-168, go to p. 752 and start reading!

These published Calendars are accessible online at Archives.org. A search for "Report on Canadian Archives" will bring up all the volumes available. You want 1884-1889.

# Loyalist Claims and Conversion List

Loyalist Claims and Conversion List [NA MG14] 1790-1837 - Audit Office 12 and 13 are compensation claims for land and goods lost during the American Revolution - 178 reels of microfilm.

Not all Loyalists filed claims but many did and if your ancestor is among those who did, you won't want to overlook this set of records.

# Heir & Devisee Commission Papers 1777-1854

The Heir & Devisee Commission papers 1777-1854 are found online in Heritage Collection of Canadian.org.

This microfilm consists of records documenting the review and determination of claims for land brought forward by the heirs, devisees, and assignees of individuals originally located by the Crown on land, in cases where no letters patent had been issued. The First Heir and Devisee Commission was in existence between 1797 and 1805.

The digitized but unindexed collection consists of 21 microfilm reels. The reels contain various volumes of the Heir & Devisee Commission papers, starting from Volume 1 to Volume 104. Canadiana.org provides a list of each microfilm and what volume numbers are included, plus a very brief description of what is contained in the volumes. For example, the first microfilm H 1143 contains Volumes 1 to 6. Volume 5, as an example, is said to contain Notices of claims, received but disallowed or unresolved, arranged alphabetically for the Eastern District ca 1809-1841.

This is very useful to the researcher as we can narrow our browsing to those microfilms of interest to us. It's still a long task as there are no indexes and each Volume is arranged differently. Some are alphabetical, some are by district and so on. But this listing of microfilms with volumes contained narrows our search. Each microfilm has been digitized and is available for immediate browsing.

Unfortunately Canadiana.org's listings are incorrect. I discovered this accidentally by searching for a specific time period in a specific location. Using the list of microfilms with contents, I chose the appropriate images. But as I scrolled through I realized something was wrong. I seemed to be looking at documents for the Johnston District, not Niagara area. Then I came across what I call a cover page - a typewritten sheet stating what Volume number I was about to view and a description of what images came next. But the volume number was wrong and should not have been on that particular microfilm according to the list provided by Canadiana.org.

I have conducted a methodical search of every microfilm that has been digitized and placed online. Of the 21 available microfilms, 10 are incorrectly identified as to volume numbers and content contained.

Here is my corrected list of microfilm reel contents, listing each film # followed by the Canadiana.org Volume list and my corrected volume if Canadiana.org's are incorrect. Those films marked with an * are incorrectly identified on Canadiana.org

H 1133; V 1-6; V 1-6
H 1134; V 6-8; V 6-8
* H 1135; V 9-15; V 16-20
* H 1136; V 16-20; V 20-24
* H 1137; V 20-24; V 24-28
* H 1138; V 24-28; V 28-32
* H 1139; V 28-32; V 33-37
* H 1140; V 33-37; V 38-44
* H 1141; V 37-44; V 45-46
* H 1142; V 46-51; V 9-15
H 1143; V 51-54; No V# labels but it is V 51-54
H 1144; V 54-63; No V# labels at start but V 56-62 labelled. This is V 54-63
H 1145; V 64-73; V 64-73
H 1146; V 74-78; V 74-78
H 1147; V 78-80; V 78-80

H 1148; V 81-83; V 81-83
H 1149; V 84-86; V 84-86
* H 1150; V 87-89; V 90-98
* H 1151; V 90-98; V 86-89
H 1152; V 99-103; V 99-103
H 1153; V 103-104; V 103-104

To assist other genealogists and researchers, I have begun providing a detailed listing of what is contained in each film along with the image number for each topic. The list can be found on my website at

http://www.olivetreegenealogy.com/can/ont/heir-devisee-commission.shtml

# Upper Canada Sundries

The Upper Canada Sundries, aka Civil Secretary's Correspondence are found at LAC (Library and Archives Canada) and at the Ontario Archives. They consist of 32 volumes on 14 reels of microfilm and are an assorted collection of, as the name implies, correspondence.

The main responsibility of the Civil or private Secretary to the Lieutenant Governor was management of correspondence. The Secretary ensured that it was acknowledged, referred onward or filed. Closely related were the duties of receiving and acknowledging Addresses, petitions, memorials and applications for office; transmitting Messages and public documents to the Legislature; and referring petitions to the appropriate public offices for opinion or advice prior to submission to the Executive Council.

Although the province of Upper Canada did not come into existence until 1791, supporting documents of earlier date have been incorporated into some series of its records.

The Sundries are filed chronologically. There is no name index but the wealth of genealogical information makes them worthwhile to browse through. They contain an assortment of such genealogical items as undated petitions, marriage certificates, land records, letters, petitions for land, testimonies during wartime, military records, petitions for mercy for those charged with treason, etc.

## An Example

I found this document during a lengthy search of the Upper Canada Sundries. It concerns the daughter of my Loyalist Ancestor Isaac Van Valkenburg aka Vollick. It reads as follows with my notes inside square brackets [ ]:

*This will testify that Albert Hainer a Private in the late Corps of Rangers [referring to Butler's Rangers, whose disbanded soldiers settled the Niagara area of present day Ontario], is married to Catharine Folluck [sic. More commonly written as Vollick or Follick], the daughter of Isaac Follluck, likewise a soldier in said Corps and that she comes under the description of a Loyalists Daughter, and is entitled [can't read next word] U.E. [Unity of Empire, a title applied to Loyalists once they were accepted by the Council and officially declared a Loyalist] and that said Albert Hainer now has five children.*

*Dated Newark, 14 May 1796.*

*Source: FHL 1683290 p. 137 of Civil Secretary's Correspondence, upper Canada, Upper Canada Sundries 1791-1800 RG5 A1 Vol. 1A pp41-556.*

It has some pretty amazing genealogy information! I have more proof that my Loyalist ancestor Isaac was in Butler's Rangers, that he had a daughter Catherine who married Albert Hainer before May 1796 and that Albert and Catherine had 5 children by that date. This document also tells me that Albert was also a soldier in Butler's Rangers and that Catherine's father has been approved as a Loyalist (as per her being allowed the title of U.E. after her name)

# State Submissions to Upper Canada 1791-1841

This series of records consists of submissions to the Executive Council on state business. It includes miscellaneous correspondence, petitions, reports, and other documents that were submitted to the Executive Council for its consideration during the period 1791-1841.

There is no index to these records, but there is a 232 page Finding Aid, and a chart which converts the details found in the Finding Aid to the correct reel of microfilm.

Heritage Canada has digitized all 20 films so let me walk you through how to figure out what film you need.

**Step One:** Finding Aid 901 can be downloaded from Library and Archives Canada with this link:
http://data2.archives.ca/pdf/pdf001/p000001750.pdf

A Conversion chart is found at the start of the Finding Aid (p. 4 of 232) This chart will help you find what reel of film you need to view the full record.

The Finding Aid is not searchable. The only way you can find a person or record of interest is to start reading!

```
M 3      1820     Petition of Matthias Brown and his wife
                  Mary Kuck for permission to return to
                  Upper Canada;  report of W. Allan on it 48A  7-13
```

*An example of a record found in the Finding Aid for State Submissions to Upper Canada 1791-1841*

**Step Two:** Once you find a record, either write down or take a screenshot of the details. In the image at the top of the page you see the bundle reference "M3" followed by the year "1820" On the bottom right you see the Volume "48A" and the page numbers "7-13"

**Step Three:** Scroll back to the Conversion Chart starting on p. 5 of the Finding Aid.  Look for your bundle, Volume and pages from the Finding Aid. You will easily find M 1-26 (M3 fits in this group); 48A, pages 1-152 followed by the film reel number 1195

**Step Four:** Now all you need to do is go to the digitized films for this set of records. The films are found on Heritage Canada. Choose Reel 1195. Then look for the page numbers you want. In this example you want to find pages 7-13.

This is where it gets a bit challenging. If you look carefully at the list of volumes that are found on Reel 1195 you will see that the reel starts with page 136 which is part of K. But you want M.  By doing a quick mental tally of all the pages that are on Reel 1195 before the section you want (M page 7) you can see that it is quite near the end of the film, about 200 pages (images) back.

There are 1590 pages (Images) on this reel. Within a few minutes I found Mathias Brown's petition to return to Canada on image 1361.

# UK, American Loyalist Claims 1776-1835

PUBLIC RECORD OFFICE, LONDON

GROUP..... *Audit office*     A.O.

CLASS ..... *Claims, American Loyalists, Series II*     13

NUMBER ..... *140*     140

CONTENTS..... *Miscellaneous*

*1801 - 1835*

There is a database online on Ancestry.com called UK, American Loyalist Claims 1776-1835. The description given by Ancestry reads "Records in this database relate to Loyalist claims and cases heard by the American Loyalist Claims Commission."

The records are divided into Series I (AO12) and Series II (AO13). It sounds wonderful and there are many images with names. But don't be misled.

While there are some Loyalist claims and documents in this set of records, a very quick look in Series II (AO 13) reveals that in the section titled "American-Loyalist Claims Series II (140) Miscellaneous 1801-1835", we find Claims for Losses in Upper Canada after the War of 1812.

These claims for losses were not filed by Loyalists but by ordinary citizens who suffered at the hands of the Americans or the Indians during that War. This specific list of those filing claims is dated May 1824 and begins on image 15 of 228. It ends on image 49 at claimant number 2054.

So use the database to search for your Loyalist ancestor but be sure you know what you are looking at when you find a name of interest.

# Carleton Papers – Loyalists and British Soldiers, 1772-1784

Library and Archives Canada website explains that The *British Headquarters Papers, New York* (also known as the *Carleton Papers*) contain records kept by commanders-in-chief of the British Army in North America during the American Revolution (1776–1783).

These 30,000 manuscript pages provide details of the services, sufferings and forced emigration of Loyalists of all classes who were banished, had their property confiscated and lived under laws of proscription because they had adhered to a lost cause.

Library and Archives Canada (LAC) holds a microfilm copy of the papers (MG23 B1, microfilms M–343 to M–369). There is a searchable database online at http://www.bac-lac.gc.ca/eng/discover/military-heritage/loyalists/loyalists-british-soldiers-1722-1784/Pages/search.aspx

A search may turn up your Loyalist ancestor in Upper Canada. For example I searched for men in Butler's Rangers, which is the regiment my Loyalist ancestors joined. There were several results, including one for Jacob Bowman in 1783 stating he was on a list of destitute persons.

www.ingramcontent.com/pod-product-compliance
Lightning Source LLC
Chambersburg PA
CBHW041226270326
41934CB00001B/13